The Post

PIANO SOLO

MUSIC FROM THE MOTION PICTURE SOUNDTRACK

ISBN 978-1-5400-2617-0

7777 W. BLUEMOUND RD. P.O. BOX 13819 MILWAUKEE, WI 53213

In Australia Contact:
Hal Leonard Australia Pty. Ltd.
4 Lentara Court
Cheltenham, Victoria, 3192 Australia
Email: ausadmin@halleonard.com.au

Visit Hal Leonard Online at
www.halleonard.com

THE PRESSES ROLL

By JOHN WILLIAMS

Moderately fast

molto rit.

SETTING THE TYPE

By JOHN WILLIAMS

THE OAK ROOM, 1971

By JOHN WILLIAMS

Moderately slow

Pedal ad lib. throughout

TWO MARTINI LUNCH

By JOHN WILLIAMS

DECIDING TO PUBLISH

By JOHN WILLIAMS

THE COURT'S DECISION AND END CREDITS

By JOHN WILLIAMS

Tempo I

MOTHER AND DAUGHTER

By JOHN WILLIAMS

Slowly, freely

Pedal ad lib. throughout